I made that

written by
Susannah Blake

WAYLAND

Revamp your room!

SAFETY ADVICE

When you make any of the projects in this book, always put safety first. Be extremely careful with sharp scissors, needles and pins and ask an adult if you need any help.

Learn stitches
Pages 110–111

Beanbag
bookends
Page 8

Styling your wardrobe

Learn stitches
Pages 110–111

Slipper chic
Page 52

Accessorising that look

Learn stitches
Pages 110–111

Daisy button
brooch
Page 64

Pampering yourself

Learn stitches
Pages 110–111

Luscious
lip balm
Page 90

Bedroom makeover

All these fab crafts are made from stuff that usually gets chucked out!

The world of interior design is a fickle thing, with yesterday's must-have becoming today's throw-away. But it needn't be that way! This book shows you the art of upcycling by using clever tricks to transform something old into something stylish and new.

Dapper decorations and fashionable furnishings

From bunting, door signs and wall art to cushions, book ends and doorstops, there's no end to the bedroom accessories that you can make from recycled materials. Reuse fabrics from old clothes, bedding and curtains. Reclaim beads and baubles from broken or discarded jewellery, snip buttons and sequins off old clothes, save ribbons from gifts and packaging, and leftover wool from knitting projects or an unravelled jumper or scarf. Set aside decorative paper such as used wrapping paper, magazines, newspapers and stationery that you could recycle and use again.

As well as being great for your room, the crafts in this book make super presents!

Funky furniture

Furniture that is perfect for reclaiming, renovating and revamping is all too often thrown on the landfill heap and rejected in favour of something brand new. So stop that trend and make it work for you! Furniture can be repainted or refreshed and decorated with scrap paper (see page 18). An old armchair or sofa can be covered with a pretty throw. And simply redressing an old bed with a bright quilt and funky cushions can transform a bedroom.

You may have furniture already that you can bring back to life with some clever crafting, but if you don't, there are lots of places to search out pre-loved pieces. Start off by looking in car boot sales, charity shops and second-hand furniture stores. The internet can also be a great source of inspiration. You will find websites advertising other people's unwanted goods and cheap online furniture auctions. In all cases, make sure you have an adult's permission and help when revamping your house and sourcing furniture.

Don't be trashy — recycle!

Beanbag bookends

K eep your books in order with these funky beanbag bookends! You can make the beanbags using fabric from old clothes, and decorate them with reclaimed ribbons and buttons. You can use a bag of rice, lentils or dried beans that's out of date and no good for cooking. They're ideal for filling the beanbags.

You will need

- ★ scissors
- ★ ruler
- ★ sturdy fabric, such as denim or corduroy
- ★ needle and thread
- ★ scrap fabric
- ★ ribbon
- ★ buttons
- ★ dried beans, lentils or grains, for filling
- ★ funnel

1

Cut out 12 10 cm x 10 cm squares from the sturdy fabric.

2

Cut out shapes, such as hearts or butterflies, from the denim or any other fabric you may have. Sew the shapes on to at least two of the squares, along with ribbons and buttons to decorate. (See pages 110–111 for sewing tips.)

3

Choose six squares for each bookend. Lay four of the squares in a row and place a square on each side of the strip to make a cross shape. Then flip each square so that the back of the fabric is showing.

4

Use a running stitch (see page 110) to sew the edges of the squares together. Leave an inch open on the final seam.

5

Turn the cube right way round, so that all the seams are on the inside. Then use a funnel to fill with beans, lentils or grains.

6

Sew up the final seam, tucking the edges in.

The more squares you decorate, the more different looks you can create. Simply rotate the bookends each day to find the design that suits your mood!

Dear diary...

Create your very own personal journal that fastens shut with a clever button and ribbon tie to keep your secrets safe. Collect unused scrap paper that's suitable for writing on for the inside pages, such as envelopes, coloured wrapping paper and old packaging. Scraps of fabric or felt from old clothes are ideal for decorating the cover.

You will need

- ★ scissors
- ★ card from a cereal packet
- ★ sturdy fabric or denim
- ★ scraps of fabric or felt, ribbons and buttons to decorate
- ★ needle and thread
- ★ fabric glue
- ★ plain scrap paper
- ★ hole punch
- ★ button(s) and ribbon to fasten the diary with

1

Cut the card into two 22 cm x 31 cm rectangles. Then cut out two 25 cm x 34 cm pieces of sturdy fabric. Sew scraps of fabric, ribbons and buttons onto one of them to decorate. Sew a large button (or two on top of each other) on the right hand side of the decorated cover.

2

Use fabric glue to stick each piece of fabric to a card rectangle, folding the fabric over to make a neat edge. Leave to dry completely. Then stick a smaller rectangle of card on to cover the glued edges.

Paper recycling

Even though paper is easily recycled, much of it ends up in landfill. What many people don't realise is that paper can take between five and 15 years to break down.

As the paper decomposes in landfills it can create methane gas, which is highly combustible and dangerous.

3

Cut the scrap paper into 15 cm x 21 cm rectangles, then stack them neatly. Working with a few pieces of paper at a time, punch six holes along one edge. Make sure that the holes are in the same position on all the pieces of paper.

4

Insert the pages between the front and back cover, ensuring the holes match up. Sew through the cardboard and the holes in the paper to bind the book together (see page 111).

5

Tie a ribbon around the book and fasten it into place by looping it around the button.

Use a thread colour that contrasts nicely with the colour of the cover.

You can reuse this diary over and over again — just cut the thread, repace the pages and sew everything back together.

Personalised door sign

Let everyone know who sleeps here with this funky personalised door sign! You only need a DVD case, photos and scrap paper. Be super chic by choosing colours that match your bedroom décor.

You will need

★ DVD case
★ scissors
★ scrap paper, such as wrapping paper, coloured card or magazines
★ photos
★ 40cm string or ribbon

1 Remove the original paper sleeve from the DVD case. Use it as a template to cut out a piece of scrap paper that is slightly smaller, and one that is the same size.

2 Decorate the smaller piece of paper with shapes cut out of scrap paper. Alternatively, you might want to make a collage with photos of family and friends, or a big picture of yourself with some pretty shapes. When you are finished decorating, stick this piece of paper onto the one that is the same size as the DVD sleeve.

Recycling photographs

Photographic paper can't be recycled like other paper products. The chemicals used in the paper and thin layer of polythene that coats the photo clog up the recycling process at paper mills.

Although this is bad news in one way, it gives you loads of opportunities to be really creative in making the most of your photos in projects such as this one.

12

3

Slide this new sleeve into the DVD case, then lay the string or ribbon along the spine. Snap the case shut and tie the ends of the string or ribbon together to make a hanging loop.

It's amazing what you can find lying around. We even used an old map for these heart shapes!

If you decide to cut up some of your old photos, make sure you ask a grown up first — they might like to keep them!

4 Hang the sign on your bedroom door!

Pretty as a picture

Finding a picture frame

If you don't have a picture frame at home, look out for one in charity shops and car boot sales. They're a great place to hunt out pre-loved items for you to recycle and revamp and usually cost very little.

Become an artist and create your very own artwork for your bedroom. Take an old picture frame and create a brand new picture to go inside it using scrap paper, such as graph paper, old envelopes, magazines and newspapers.

You will need

- ★ sandpaper (optional)
- ★ acrylic paint
- ★ paintbrush
- ★ scrap paper, buttons
- ★ glue
- ★ scissors
- ★ card from a cereal packet

1

Carefully remove the back and glass from the picture frame. You may want to sand the frame to make the paint stick to it well. Then paint with acrylic paint and leave to dry.

2

Cut out a piece of paper to fit inside the frame. Create a collage picture by glueing shapes on top, leaving plenty of space around the outside for a mount.

3

To make a mount, cut out a piece of card the same size as the picture. Mark a rectangle inside leaving a border of at least 2 cm. Cut out the centre to create the mount.

4

Paint the mount in a colour that goes well with those used in the picture. Set it aside to dry.

5

Place the mount on the picture, then slip into the frame and clip back together. Hang it on your bedroom wall!

Buttoned wool cushion

This project is a fantastic way to give a new lease of life to an old cardigan. The buttoned front gives a stylish finish with almost no effort at all! Use an old cushion or cushion pad for the filling.

You will need
★ an old buttoned cardigan
★ cushion pad
★ dress-making pins
★ scissors
★ needle and thread

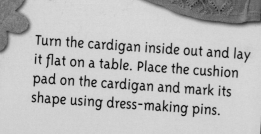

1 Turn the cardigan inside out and lay it flat on a table. Place the cushion pad on the cardigan and mark its shape using dress-making pins.

2 Cut around the pins to make the basic cushion shape. Make sure you leave a border around the pins of about 2 cm.

Never throw your worn-out jumpers away. Even if they have holes you can still recycle the wool.

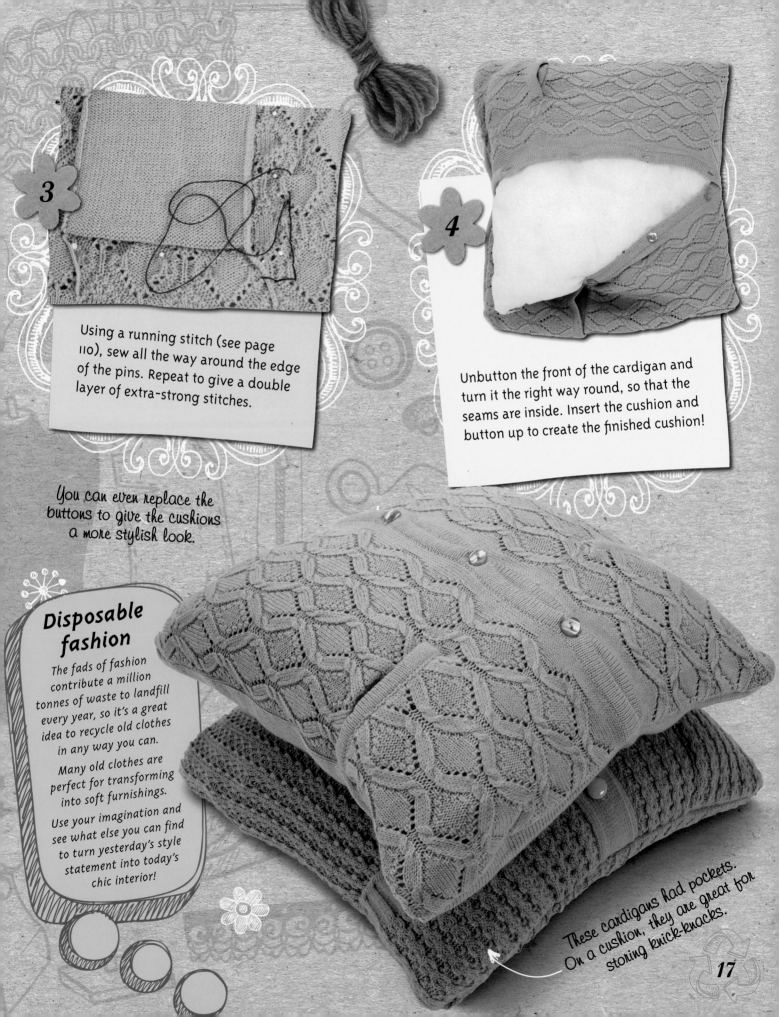

3

Using a running stitch (see page 110), sew all the way around the edge of the pins. Repeat to give a double layer of extra-strong stitches.

4

Unbutton the front of the cardigan and turn it the right way round, so that the seams are inside. Insert the cushion and button up to create the finished cushion!

You can even replace the buttons to give the cushions a more stylish look.

Disposable fashion

The fads of fashion contribute a million tonnes of waste to landfill every year, so it's a great idea to recycle old clothes in any way you can.

Many old clothes are perfect for transforming into soft furnishings.

Use your imagination and see what else you can find to turn yesterday's style statement into today's chic interior!

These cardigans had pockets. On a cushion, they are great for storing knick-knacks.

Bedroom cabinet

Upcycle your tired old bedroom cabinet and turn it into the centrepiece of your room! All you need is a little paint and some scrap paper. Search out coloured scrap paper such as magazines, newspapers, junk mail, leaflets and flyers that will complement the other colours in your bedroom. Before you start, check that you are allowed to renovate the cabinet!

2

Cut the scrap paper into shapes. You might want to use them to create a little scene or a colourful collage.

1

If necessary, lightly sand the bedside cabinet to help the paint stick to the surface. Then paint with acrylic paint and leave to dry.

The paint will cover better if you use a lighter shade of paint as an undercoat. Perhaps you have some that needs using up?

3

When the cabinet is completely dry, stick the shapes on in your chosen design using PVA glue.

4

Paint a thin layer of PVA glue over the whole cabinet to seal your design and leave to dry completely.

We painted this cabinet using tester pots. You can get these for free or very little money in DIY shops.

Furniture dump

Research by the Furniture Reuse Network has shown that local councils in the UK send around 10 million reusable items of furniture to landfill in a single year.

Bunting!

Nothing cheers up a bedroom like a string of bunting! Whether it's in bright colours or seaside stripes, bunting is a great way to add a touch of fun to your room. Pick out some old clothes that don't fit you anymore so that you can turn happy memories into funky interior fashion.

You will need

★ an old pair of jeans
★ scrap material from old clothes
★ ribbon or string
★ scissors
★ needle and thread

1 Cut the jeans into triangles (about 25 cm high and 20 cm wide). You will need at least five triangles, and it is ideal to end up with an odd, rather than an even number.

25 cm

2 Cut out shapes or letters from the scrap material. You can make their edges look pretty by adding a blanket stitch (see page 111).

3

Sew the shapes onto the triangles. If you have beads, you can attach them to the bottom of each triangle.

4

Sew the top of each triangle to the ribbon with about 3 cm between each one. If you only have short bits of ribbon, sew them together to make one long piece before attaching the triangles.

Broken beads

If you break a necklace or bracelet, don't despair. Pick up the beads and store them in a jar. They'll be great for adding decoration to bunting or similar furnishings, such as cushions or mobiles.

You can personalise your bunting by spelling your name across it!

Box of treasures

Whether you need a jewellery box to keep your beads and bangles in, or just a special place to store your favourite things, this beautiful box is a must for every bedroom.

1

Coat the lid of the shoe box in a thin layer of PVA glue and cover with strips of scrap paper. Leave to dry completely.

If you dont have any coloured or patterned paper, you can try cutting up magazines.

2

Place the small cardboard boxes inside the shoe box to create compartments within the box. If necessary, cut down the height of the boxes so that they fit inside the shoe box.

Repackage your packaging

Food and consumer goods create a vast amount of waste due to packaging. Often goods are contained within several layers of packaging. This may be to protect the product on its long journey to the consumer, but these numerous layers of packaging also find their way to the growing heaps of landfill. How many different ways can you think of to reclaim and reuse this excess packaging?

3

Use the scrap paper to decorate the boxes. Then stick them inside the shoe box.

4

Use the ribbon to wrap around the box and fasten it shut.

To make these cute butterflies, just layer butterfly shapes in different sizes and colours and stick their centre to the box.

You can use your box to collect fabric, buttons and ribbons that you might like to use for other projects.

Cute CD hanger

Damaged or used CDs are tricky things to recycle, but not to re-use as decoration. This cute hanger will add a bit of sparkle to any boudoir!

You will need

★ 5-7 old CDs
★ scrap paper or magazines
★ pencil
★ scissors
★ glue
★ ribbon
★ sticky tape
★ beads

2

Cut out pretty flower shapes and stick them onto the circles.

1

Using a CD as a template, draw circles on the backs of scrap paper or magazine images and cut them out.

3

Stick the decorated circles onto the CDs.

4

Add beads to one end of the ribbon and tie a knot. If you only have short pieces of ribbon, use a needle and thread to sew them together to make a piece long enough for your CDs.

5

Make a loop at the other end of the ribbon, then stick the ribbon to the backs of the CDs with sticky tape. Now it's ready to hang up!

Why not have pictures of your best freinds in the centre of your CD flowers?

Window mobile

Take nature as your inspiration to make this beautiful leafy mobile. Watch the leaves spin in the breeze, and reflect the sunshine on their shiny surface. At night they will shine in the glow of the lightbulb in your bedroom lamp.

1 Wind wool or embroidery thread around the CD to cover the shiny surface.

2 Cut the scrap paper into leaf shapes. You can make them all kinds of different shapes and sizes.

Making the most of old CDs

Pass CDs on to someone else who might enjoy them, or give them to a charity shop. Sell them at a car boot sale or put an ad in your local corner shop. Alternatively, these shining discs are great for scaring away birds when hung over your veggie patch or in fruit trees. Whatever you do, don't just throw them away – look for a new home or use for them.

People throw away lots of old CDs. If you haven't got any yourself, ask around!

3

Carefully cover both sides of each leaf with sticky tape. Snip away any excess tape.

If you use tissue paper for your leaves, the light will shine through them like stained glass.

4

Using the hole punch, stamp a hole in the top of each leaf. Then attach each of them to a piece of wool or embroidery thread.

5

Attach the leaves to the CD using a slightly longer piece of wool or thread for each one. Fix four equal lengths of wool to the top of the CD and knot the ends together to hang up your mobile.

Owl door stop

Make this cute owl door stop to keep your door open... or closed! Use an old pillow case or fabric from a shirt, dress or skirt. If you like dress-making or sewing, you may have some suitable scraps left over from a previous project. An old cushion or puffy jacket are ideal sources of wadding.

2

Cut out shapes from scrap fabric to make the background for the face, the eyes, the beak and the feathers. Sew the shapes onto the front of the pillowcase and add two (or four) buttons for the eyes.

1

Cut the pillowcase in half and reserve the closed end. You can use the open end for another project.

3

Fill the bottom of the pillowcase with a layer of lentils, rice or dried beans, then fill the rest with wadding. Sew across the top to enclose the filling materials.

4

Tie the two top corners using some thread to create ears.

Make the most of your storecupboard

If you don't keep track of your storecupboard staples such as couscous, lentils or rice, you can easily find that a packet has gone past its sell-by date. Rather than throwing it away, why not use the old grains or pulses for craft projects like this one.

5

Depending on the design of the cushion cover you have, you could make a dog, a cat or any other animal to guard your door!

You can also make mini owls out of the leftover cushion cover to use as paper weights.

Style your bedroom!

Transforming your room by using new accessories and colour is one of the best ways of expressing yourself. And the good news is, it doesn't need to be wasteful or contribute to the ever-growing mountains of landfill. By recycling, reclaiming and reusing you can make everything out of nothing and give a new lease of life to items that might otherwise have ended up on the rubbish tip.

Make it all about you

Think about colours you like and reclaim, recycle and reuse materials in those shades to create a coordinated look. Or if you prefer a hodge-podge of colour and pattern, embrace your quirky side and go for it!

Once you've decided on these basics, think about what kind of bedroom accessories you need. Do you need a desk for doing homework? Do you need a dressing table for trying out new hairstyles? Do you need bookends to keep your books in order and a diary to write down all your personal thoughts? Do you need cushions and beanbags to hang out on with your friends?

Embrace your own interior style

Have the confidence in your own likes and dislikes and create a look that's true to your own taste and style. To develop your own style and explore what you like, find inspiration on the internet or from books and magazines. There are hundreds of different looks out there, for example, there's art deco, English country, French country, industrial and colonial. You can take elements from what you see and create your own unique style.

This box of treasures looks fab, but there are so many other ways you could decorate it — paint, foils, or even glitter!

Reuse your skills

Once you've mastered the basic projects in this book, think about how you could reuse those skills for new projects. Redecorate other items of furniture using the techniques used for the bedside cabinet on pages 18–19, or make a notebook in the same way as the diary on pages 10–11. You could also make a selection of cushions similar to the one on pages 16–17 using other clothes with fastenings, such as a zip-up top or a buttoned shirt.

The only limit to restyling your room is your imagination!

Eco-Fashion

It's the new buzz word on the front rows of fashion week, but what does eco-fashion really mean? Any fashion that takes into account the environment, the health of consumers (that's you!) and the working conditions of people employed in the fashion industry is part of the eco-fashion scene. And right now, that's the place to be!

Fashion and the environment

When buying new clothes or fashion accessories, look for ones made from eco-friendly raw materials. That means fabrics made from organic materials such as cotton that have been grown without the use of pesticides, and that have been coloured without the use of harmful bleaches or dyes. Also look out for clothes that make use of reused and reclaimed materials.

Make sure you save any pretty buttons or sequins from worn out clothes.

Create your own eco-fashion

Making your own trend statement by creating clothes and accessories out of reused, recycled, reclaimed and pre-loved materials instantly plants you firmly in the eco-fashion scene. Whether you're revamping an old jacket or cardigan with pretty ribbons and buttons or making a cool new scarf from scratch — as long as you're reusing, you're bang on trend!

Find your own inspiration

The secret behind really successful eco-styling is having an eye for the right materials. The first place to look is around the home, starting with your own wardrobe, then asking your family, friends and relatives. You can also check out second-hand clothes and accessories in charity shops.

Look out for fabrics and colours that you love. If clothes are worn out or too small, don't just throw them away. Snip off the buttons, save sequins, beads or ribbons, and hold on to knits. Even old blankets and curtains have the potential to be turned into something fabulous!

Tie~d together belt

You will need

★ 1 belt
★ 3 ties
★ needle and thread
★ 1 button

Use an old belt to make a new one! Remove the old buckle from a belt and attach it to a gorgeous new strap made from silky ties. You can even use the belt strap for another project, such as a strap for a new handbag!

2 Lay the ties on top of each other and feed the slim ends through the belt buckle.

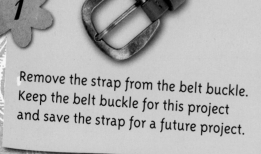

1 Remove the strap from the belt buckle. Keep the belt buckle for this project and save the strap for a future project.

How to remove a belt buckle

A fabric or fake leather belt strap can be cut off using a pair of scissors. A leather belt strap may be attached with a popper, stud or stitching. For a stud, you will need to ask an adult to help you prise the stud open. If the belt is stitched, snip and unpick the stitches using a small pair of pointed scissors.

Leather belts can be tough, so take care when cutting them.

3 Use a running stitch (page 30) to hold the buckle in place.

4

Plait the ties.

Why stop at just one belt? You could make a range of belts to complement your wardrobe.

5 Sew the ends of the ties together with a pretty button. Use the gaps in the plaited strap to fasten the buckle in place around your waist.

This belt would work just as well tied around your favourite dress.

Reusable bag

Instead of using a plastic bag when you go shopping, always make sure you've got this handy pack-away bag tucked into your handbag. It's cool, gorgeous and good for the environment – and with eco-style in mind, it's only going to add to your fashion cred!

1

Cut two 30 cm x 45 cm rectangles from the heavy fabric. Cut two long strips, 60 cm x 10 cm, from the same fabric.

2

We chose to decorate our bag with leaves and flowers. For the flowers, cut out rounded crosses from the felt (see below), and pinch them together in the centre. Sew the pinched felt together.

Flowers and leaves look great in felt, but you could use hearts, butterflies or stars, too.

Drastic plastic

The average plastic bag is used for just five minutes, but takes about 500 years to decompose. Billions are used every year and end up littering streets and parks as well as pointlessly filling landfill sites. Plastic bags are dangerous, too, as they can kill birds and small mammals.

3

Once you have created your decorations, sew them onto one of the fabric rectangles. We used buttons to attach the flowers.

4

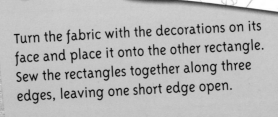

Turn the fabric with the decorations on its face and place it onto the other rectangle. Sew the rectangles together along three edges, leaving one short edge open.

5

Fold both long strips in half, lengthwise. Sew along the edges, leaving one short edge open. Then turn the fabric inside out. These will form the handles of the bag.

6

Fold back the open edges of the rectangles and sew them, creating a hem. Turn the rectangles inside out and sew the ends of the handles to the hemmed edges.

Your bag is ready for its first shopping trip!

Mac makeover

Upcycle your drab old winter mac or coat and turn it into something fabulous using scraps of old ribbon and home-made paper beads.

You will need

★ old mac or jacket
★ brightly coloured tissue paper
★ water
★ PVA glue
★ bamboo skewer
★ coloured felt and buttons (optional)
★ needle and thread
★ decorative fabric or ribbon

1 Remove any boring or broken buttons from the mac, and remove the belt if it has one.

2 Tear the tissue paper into small pieces and soak in water for about one hour, until very soft. Squeeze out most of the water, then mix in just enough PVA glue to make a thick paste. Shape the pulp into buttons and make two holes into the centre of them, using a bamboo skewer.

3 Leave the buttons to dry in a warm place until hard. This may take a few days. Then sew them onto your mac in place of the old buttons.

If you don't have any coloured tissue paper, make plain butons and paint them when they have dried.

38

4

Sew strips of fabric or ribbon onto the collars, cuff and pockets to make a smart trim. You can use the same ribbon or fabric as a belt.

5

Make a cute brooch for your upcycled mac by cutting out shapes from the felt. You can layer the shapes and create a trim using a blanket stitch (page 111). Sew the shapes onto your mac using pretty buttons.

Recycling ribbons

Silky ribbons are perfect for this project. You'll find them in all kinds of places – from gift wrapping and chocolate boxes to packaging for cosmetics. Keep your eyes peeled and always save any scraps you find so you've got a great selection to choose from.

Wow! How lovely does this fab 'new' mac look?

Scarf sensation

Getting woolly

If you know a knitter, ask them for any old balls of leftover wool they may have, or check out your local charity shop. Alternatively, unravel an old jumper or scarf. The wool will have lots of kinks and bends that will add to the fascinating texture of your pom poms!

Why make do with a boring old knitted scarf when you could have this fantastic fluffy pom pom scarf instead! Make it using leftover wool from a knitting project or reclaimed wool from an old jumper. Card from a cereal box is perfect for making the pom poms.

You will need

★ pencil
★ card
★ scissors
★ wool in different colours
★ compass
★ needle

1

Using a compass, draw two circles with a diameter of 9 cm. Then draw another circle inside each round with a diameter of 5 cm. Cut each of these rings out.

2

Place the card rings together. Wrap a few layers of wool around the rings.

3

Carefully snip around the outside of the rings, cutting through the wool loops.

4

Tie a length of wool between the two card rings to secure the wool loops. Tie the wool length in a tight knot and remove the card rings to reveal a fluffy wool pom pom.

5

Make at least 15 pom poms. Then, using a needle, thread them onto a long length of plaited wool to create your scarf.

Wool comes from animals such as sheep or alpacas. The animals are sheared, and the fleece is then cleaned and spun into the threads we use to make clothes.

41

Gilet glamour

Get the festival vibe with this stylish boho gilet! All you need is an old cardigan, some funky buttons and beads, and wool to create a tassled fringe.

1 Cut the sleeves off the cardigan about 2 cm from the seam, then fray the edges by cutting into them with a pair of scissors. Snip off any old buttons.

2 Cut 7 cm lengths of wool. Fold a length in two, then poke the loop through a hole in the knitting around the arm hole. Tuck the cut ends through the loop and pull tight to produce a tassel.

Broken beads

There's nothing so disappointing as breaking a favourite necklace and watching the beads roll away and get lost. But don't despair! Hold on to the remaining beads and use them in a project like this one. That way you can carry on enjoying your favourite necklace... even though it's not a necklace anymore!

3

Sew the new buttons onto the cardigan.

4

Using a tapestry needle and wool, sew beads onto the hems of the cardigan pockets. Use a whipping stitch (see page III), threading a bead on with every stitch.

5

Sew strings of beads and bead tassles around the hem of the gillet to create a boho-style finish.

Perfect poncho

This South American classic is a great alternative to a conventional coat. Not only is it bang on trend, it's incredibly easy to make using an old blanket, decorated with embroidery and a beaded fringe. Save beads from old or broken necklaces and re-thread them to create your poncho decorations.

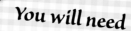

1 Cut the blanket into a 1 metre x 1 metre square. Use thread or wool to sew around the edges in blanket stitch (see page 110).

2 Fold two corners of the blanket together to make a triangle shape. Then snip a 'T' shape (approximately 20 cm long) in the centre for your head to go through. Use thread or wool to sew around the edges in blanket stitch.

Make your own blanket

If you don't have a blanket to use for this project, make your own patchwork blanket. You can do this by sewing together squares of scrap fabric from old clothes.

4

Thread beads on to lengths of wool to make 5 cm-long tassels. Sew them onto the corners of the poncho.

3

Cut shapes out of felt and decorate them with sequins. You can sew around the edges of the shapes in blanket stitch. Sew them onto the poncho.

Traditional ponchos have been worn for many hundreds of years in South America.

Why not try making a traditional poncho for fancy dress?

5

Decorate the collar of your poncho by sewing on lots of pretty buttons.

Groovy shoes

Clean up a grubby old pair of canvas pumps and transform them into something new and fantastic by decorating with patterns and adding flash shoe laces!

1

Clean up the canvas pumps using soap and a scrubbing brush. Remove the old laces. Using a pencil, sketch pictures and patterns to create a funky all-over design.

2

Cut two pieces of ribbon to the length of the old shoelaces. Wrap sticky tape around the ends to stop them fraying.

You could ask an adult to clean your old pumps in the washing machine instead of scrubbing them.

3

Fill in the sketches with the acrylic paint. Let the paint dry for a few hours.

4

Use a permanent marker pen to trace around the edges of the shapes. Then thread ribbons through the eyelets.

Share your shoes

About 330 million pairs of shoes are thrown out every year, ending up in landfill. Revamping a pair of shoes is a great way to chip away at this wastage. There are other ways you can help too. If shoes are too small, take them to a charity shop or recycling centre, so someone else can get some wear out of them.

Customising your shoes means that they are unique as well as eco chic!

Try using coloured insulation tape for the ends to add more colour.

Transform a T-shirt

Bored of an old T-shirt and don't want to wear it any more? Give it a new lease of life by customising it in a few simple and fun steps!

1

Use a pair of scissors to remove the collar.

2

Cut shapes out of the scrap fabric to create a cute motif. You can sew around the edges of the shapes in a blanket stitch, too (see page 111).

Unwanted clothes are often dumped in landfill sites.

3

Sew the shape onto the T-shirt and add buttons to decorate.

4

Cut thin strips of fabric and fold them like a concertina. Stick a needle and thread through each bundle of folded fabric.

Why not sew on your favourite cartoon character?

Disposable fashion to landfill nightmare

The popularity of low-cost fashion that is worn and then thrown away quickly has contributed to a massive one million tonnes of textile waste every year. Take your own steps to combat this terrible wastage by reusing, recycling and reclaiming as many items of clothing as you can!

5

Pull the strips apart and sew them onto the hem of each sleeve.

A skirt to flirt!

Jazz up an ordinary skirt with a ruffled net petticoat and ribbon decorations to create the ultimate party piece!

You will need

★ tape measure
★ scissors
★ net curtains
★ needle and thread
★ skirt
★ scrap fabric

1 Measure your waist, then double this measurement. Cut three strips of net curtain to this length and each strip as wide as the length of your skirt.

2 Sew the net ruffles to the underside of the skirt using a running stitch (page 110).

You can decorate your skirt with anything from sparkly brooches and sequins to fabric paints.

50

3

Cut thin strips of scrap fabric, as well as some pretty shapes with which to decorate the skirt.

4

Sew the end of a strip of fabric to the hem of the skirt; attach a second strip to it with a bow. Then sew on that strip and carry on attaching the strips until the hem of the skirt is decorated in a line of bows.

5

Sew the shapes you cut out earlier to the front of the skirt.

Slipper chic

You will need

★ cereal packet
★ pencil
★ an old fleece top
★ needle and thread
★ buttons
★ coloured felt

You can really make your own style statement with these cute and cosy slippers. Fleece from an old jumper or hoody is the ideal fabric and looks gorgeous decorated with reclaimed buttons.

2

Place the card templates on the fleece and cut around them with a pair of scissors.

1

Put one of your shoes on the opened out cereal packet and draw around it. Cut out the shape. Repeat with your other foot.

3

Measure around the card template and note this length. Then cut out two rectangles of fleece that are of this length and 15 cm wide.

Easy felt

Felt is a brilliant fabric for making slippers and you can make your own from an old jumper. Next time there's a hot wash going into the washing machine, throw in an old wool jumper that you don't wear any more. After a few hot washes you'll find that your old jumper has taken on a matted, felty texture that's perfect for turning into something new and funky.

4

Sew one fleece strip on to one of the fleece insoles, using a blanket stitch (see page 111) to make it really secure. Repeat with the second slipper.

5

To make the slipper shape, gather the front of the slipper by sewing around the top edge of the sides with a running stitch (see page 110).

Instead of buttons, you could attach pom poms to your slippers. Flip back to pages 40–41 to see how to make them.

6

Pull the running stitch together to gather the front of your slipper and secure with a few stitches. You can sew a button onto the top to cover up the stitches.

Why not decorate the sides of your slippers with some pretty stars?

53

Dazzling jeans

You can bring a bit of sparkle to your old jeans by adding fabulous pocket patches, decorated with sequins and ribbons. Look out for sequins that you can snip off old clothes, and save those little pouches of spare sequins that often come attached to new sequinned clothes.

1

Cut a square out of felt that will fit onto your jeans back pocket.

2

Sew a decorative pattern on to the patch using sequins and ribbon.

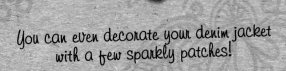

You can even decorate your denim jacket with a few sparkly patches!

3

Sew the patch onto the jeans pocket with a whipping stitch (see page 111).

(see page 111).

Go organic

Growing cotton accounts for 25 per cent of the agro-chemicals (agricultural chemicals) used in the world. Denim is made from cotton, so whenever you can, choose organic to ease the environmental load of all those chemicals.

Or you could try...

If you've ripped an old pair of jeans, why don't you save their life by repairing them with a decorative patch. Use the same technique as the one used here to create pretty patches for repairs.

If you've got a favourite top that you love to wear with your jeans, choose the same colours to make your patch to create a cool, coordinating outfit.

Find your own style

Having the confidence to create your own style with flair is a great skill to have. Fashion trends change with the season, and that's a big part of the reason why fashion can have such a negative effect on the environment. People buy clothes because they're in, then go off them a few months later when something new arrives in the shops.

By learning how to make your own style statement, you'll find you get more out of your clothes and stay on trend by knowing how to revamp, restyle and customise your look.

Your super slippers would make a great gift!

Trust your taste

Always choose clothes and fabrics in colours and prints that you love. You'll often find these colours naturally go together, making it easier for you to mix and match your wardrobe to create new look after new look.

Dare to experiment

True style icons have never been afraid to step out from the crowd. Throughout time, the real leaders in fashion have always been the first to try new looks and break the mould, rather than staying in line with the fashion herd. If you think something looks good then express your individuality and don't be afraid to show off your inner flair and style!

You can put together a collage with different fashion ideas you've seen in films, magazines, online or even sketches you've made yourself. You can pin up scraps of wool, lace, velvet or denim and fabrics with patterns that interest you. This will give you inspiration and ideas to customise your own wardrobe.

Look to the future

Today's trend used to be tomorrow's landfill, but by using the projects in this book you can keep your wardrobe fresh without any of the waste.

You could use the techniques in 'Transfom a T-shirt' on pages 48–49 to create a funky skirt or dress, or revamp a bag or top using the techniques in 'Dazzling jeans' on pages 54–55. You could even make smart felt slippers for your brother or boyfriend using the basic techniques for 'Slipper chic' on pages 52–53.

The only limits to your style are how far you can stretch your imagination!

Dazzling Jewellery

Sparkling jewellery, made of beautiful gems and precious metals, can look like a stunning work of art. But there is a darker side to the production of jewellery, especially in some of the industries that mine for metals, such as gold and platinum, or precious stones, such as rubies, emeralds and diamonds.

Jewellery ethics

Mining for valuable materials used in jewellery all too often comes at a great cost to the environment, the workers involved in their production and to the country where the gems come from. Environmental destruction through the use of dynamite and dangerous chemicals is still widespread. 'Conflict gemstones', for example diamonds or sapphires, are associated with child labour, dangerous and unregulated conditions, funding military regimes and harming the environment.

Taking responsibility

There is a growing movement among jewellery designers to only use precious metals and stones obtained through responsible mining, healthy conditions for the workers and from an area of peace. They insist on being clear about their supply chains, demanding to know where and how their metals and stones have been come by.

As well as being great additions to your jewellery box, the crafts in this book make super presents!

All these fab crafts are made from stuff that usually gets thrown out!

Pretty, not precious

Beautiful jewellery can be made from all kinds of materials, not just precious metals and stones. And by choosing to avoid materials that can cause damage to the environment you can be gorgeous and fashionable, but have a clear conscience too. Jewellery made from recycled materials is even better, transforming you into the Eco Queen of Bling!

Find your inner magpie

So what can you reclaim, reuse and recycle to make the fabulous projects in this book? First of all, you need to find your inner magpie. Look out at home, in charity shops and at car boot sales for anything shiny, sparkly, twinkly and pretty. Sequins, buttons and beads snipped off old clothes are great. Silky and shiny fabrics from old clothes, ties and furnishing materials are ideal. Fastenings and catches from clothes and broken jewellery are essential. Reworking old, broken or damaged pieces of jewellery is a must. Silk, satin, velvet and sparkly ribbon, braid and cords from packaging are always useful. And scrap paper in pretty colours and textures is endlessly versatile when it comes to designing and making your own dazzling jewellery.

Don't be trashy – recycle!

Charm bracelet

Create this truly personalised charm bracelet using small reclaimed objects such as beads, shells, pieces of broken jewellery, or an odd earring. Each object could have a special significance for you, helping to make this bracelet really special.

1

Assemble your charms and make sure they'll be easy to attach to the bracelet. If you like, you can paint some of the charms. To make sure the paint sticks well, mix a little PVA glue to the paint, then paint on and leave to dry.

2

Measure a length of ribbon or string around your wrist, making sure there's plenty of extra to tie the bracelet on, then snip it to the right length. Cut two more pieces of string or ribbon to the same length.

Recycling ribbons

You can find pretty ribbons in all kinds of places – from gift wrapping and chocolate boxes to packaging for cosmetics. Keep your eyes peeled and always save any scraps you find, so you've got a great selection to choose from!

3

Tie the three pieces of ribbon together in a knot at one end and plait them. Secure the plait with a knot at the other end.

4

Cut a piece of ribbon or string, 6 cm long, for each of the charms. Tie a knot in the end of each of the strings or ribbons and thread a charm onto each of them.

5

Tie each charm to the plaited ribbons and cut off any excess ribbon.

Make sure you ask an adult before you cut up their jewellery!

Why not colour code your charms to match your favourite outfit?

Watch that bling!

Give an old watch a new lease of life by attaching a new, groovy, sparkling strap. To decorate, you can use sequins scavenged from old clothes.

1 Remove the strap from the watch. If you can't cut the straps off, check the box below for other ways of removing them.

2 Cut two lengths of ribbon that are each between 4 and 6 cm longer than one of the old straps.

3 Sew sequins onto the ribbons to decorate.

How to remove a watch strap

Most watch straps are attached to a little bar at the top and bottom of the watch face. Find the tiny hole in line with each bar. Press a needle or pin into the hole and it should release the bar. You may need to ask an adult to help you. Once the strap is off, slip the bar back into place.

If you really can't get the strap off, pop into your local jeweller and ask them if they can remove it. It should only take a second and they shouldn't need to charge you.

62

4

Loop one length of decorated ribbon through the bar at the top of the watch and sew on securely. Repeat with the second piece of ribbon at the bottom bar.

5

Cut the string into three pieces that are each 10 cm long. Tie a knot into one end of each of them. Thread beads onto each length of string.

6

Attatch the beads to the bottom bar of the watch and cut off any excess string.

You can sew sequins onto the ribbon to cover up any stitches.

63

Daisy button brooch

Create a beautiful floral brooch using an old tie, a button and a brooch fastener. Ask your dad or granddad for any old ties and search for the perfect button on old clothes. You may need to buy a brooch fastner, unless you can use one from a brooch you don't wear anymore.

2 Fold the tie up in a concertina shape, allowing about 10 cm for each fold.

1 Cut off the wider half of the tie and set it aside for another project; you only need the narrow end to make your brooch.

3 Pinch the centre of the folded tie firmly between your thumb and forefinger and use your other hand to fan out the tie into a flower shape. Sew around the centre a few times to keep it in place.

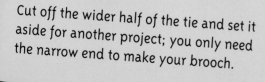

4

Sew the button into the centre of the flower.

5

Sew the brooch fastener onto the back of the flower.

Button up!

Buttons are fantastic for upcycling. You can use them to make or decorate anything from jewellery and clothes to accessories and furnishings for the home.

How many ways can you think of to reuse a button?

Why not use your brooch to decorate your favourite hat?

Flutterby fascinator

Make a dazzling, fun fascinator by decorating an old hair slide with feathers, sequins and stunning paper butterflies. Funky hair accessories are the latest trend so you'll be truly hip and happening with your hair swept back with this gorgeous hair slide.

You will need

- ★ hair slide
- ★ scrap paper
- ★ pencil
- ★ scissors
- ★ craft wire
- ★ wire cutters
- ★ craft glue
- ★ sequins
- ★ feathers
- ★ ribbon

1 Draw two butterfly shapes and a heart shape onto a piece of scrap paper. On a different coloured piece of scrap paper, draw the same shapes, just smaller. Cut out all the shapes.

2 Cut three pieces of craft wire, each about 7 cm long. Stick the pieces of wire between the smaller butterfly or heart shapes and their larger equivalents.

Sourcing decorative paper

There are so many different places to find scrap paper that's just perfect for recycling into fab fashion statements. Save scraps of pretty wrapping and tissue paper from gifts and packaging. Tear out pages from magazines where you love the colours and designs. Also always keep decorative paper bags when you've been shopping.

3

Decorate the front top part of the hair slide by glueing on sequins.

4

Glue the wired shapes to the back of the hair slide, along with some feathers.

You can stick sequins to the shapes to add more sparkle!

5

In order to keep the feathers and wire in place, stick a length of ribbon across the back of the hair slide using craft glue.

Fabulous fluffy bangle

This beautiful bangle is the perfect way to use up scraps of fabric left over from sewing projects or reclaimed from old clothes. Mining precious metals and stones can be extremely harmful to the environment so choosing to wear jewellery made from fabric means you're really doing your bit to lessen your personal impact on the environment.

You will need

★ decorative fabric
★ scissors
★ embroidery thread
★ measuring tape
★ needle
★ jewellery fastenings

1

Cut or rip the fabric into long, narrow strips. Don't worry about the strips being identical — this bangle looks better if there is a variety of fabric lengths and widths.

2

Wrap the embroidery thread around your wrist, then add about 9 cm to that length and snip. Tie a knot about 3 cm from one end and thread the other end into the needle.

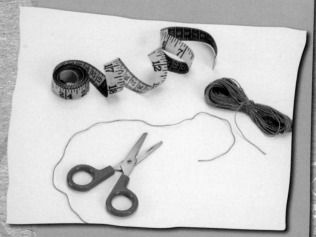

68

3

Roll each strip of fabric into a loose roll, with the pattern on the outside.

Jewellery fastenings

Always save broken necklaces and bracelets, so that you can reuse the old parts. Hook and eye loops or pull-back catches are ideal for this bracelet, so just look through your collection of broken jewellery until you find one. Snip it off and make it into something new!

4

Thread each of the fabric rolls onto the embroidery thread.

5

Attach the fastenings to the ends of the thread with a double knot.

Why not make individual bangles for your best friends — they will adore them!

Sparkling choker

This super-simple necklace makes the ultimate style statement. Chokers are very simple to create but just shout sophistication. Look out for pretty ribbons on packaging or gift wrap, or maybe you have an old hair ribbon that would also be perfect. Snip the sequins off old clothes and look out for hooks and eyes on the waistband of an old skirt.

You will need

★ velvet ribbon
★ scissors
★ sequins
★ needle and thread
★ hooks and eyes

2 Decorate the ribbon with sequins in any design you like.

1

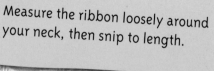
Measure the ribbon loosely around your neck, then snip to length.

3

Sew the hooks to one end and the eyes to the other.

Why not customise a party dress with sequins to match your choker?

Dazzling jewels!

Sequins are a great way to add sparkle without impacting on the environment in the way that mining for precious stones such as diamonds can. Think about the kind of look you want to go for. You could sew a simple line of sequins along the centre of the choker, or a line on each edge. You could make a pretty swirling pattern, or just go mad and cover the whole ribbon so it's sparkle, sparkle, sparkle all the way!

Pretty pendant

There's nothing worse than losing a favourite earring... but don't worry! Make this lovely pendant and you can still keep on enjoying your favourite pieces. A dangly earring will work best as you need something big and bold to make a real impact.

You will need
★ ribbon
★ single dangly earring
★ needle and thread
★ beads
★ scissors

1

Decide how low you want your pendant to hang, then cut the ribbon to length, allowing a little extra for tying the necklace on.

2

Thread the earring onto the ribbon.

No ribbon?
Can't find a piece of ribbon long enough? Never fear, you can use scrap fabric instead. Find some old clothes (checking first that you can use them) and cut out three long, narrow strips. Plait the strips together to make the cord for your necklace.

3 Cut three pieces of ribbon, all at different lengths. Tie a knot at one end of each piece of ribbon. Then use a needle to thread beads onto the ribbons.

4 Tie the ribbons to the pendant.

The earring we have used gives our pendant a lovely 'vintage chic' look!

5 As a finishing touch, tie a length of ribbon around the top of the pendant in a pretty bow.

Button Bracelet

Did you know...

Mining for precious metals often involves toxic chemicals that are dangerous both to the environment and human and animal health. Three of the main culprits that can cause contamination to water, soil and air include mercury, sulphuric acid and cyanide.

Pretty buttons are great for turning into jewellery. Whether they're made from plastic, glass, mother of pearl, wood or fabric, they're just amazing. When clothes are past their best, always have a look to see whether you can rescue any buttons. A box of multi-coloured buttons is like a miniature treasure chest!

You will need

★ scissors
★ ribbon in different colours
★ lots of buttons
★ needle and thread
★ jewellery fastenings

1

Measure ribbon around your wrist and cut to length, allowing for a few centimetres extra at each end to attach the jewellery fastenings.

2

Look through your button collection and arrange your favourite ones in a row to create a pretty visual effect. You might like to layer them, placing small buttons on top of larger ones.

74

3

Using a needle and thread, sew together any layered buttons.

4

Attach the jewellery fastenings to the ends of the measured ribbon. You could add a pretty bow, too. You can attach it by sewing it to the ribbon.

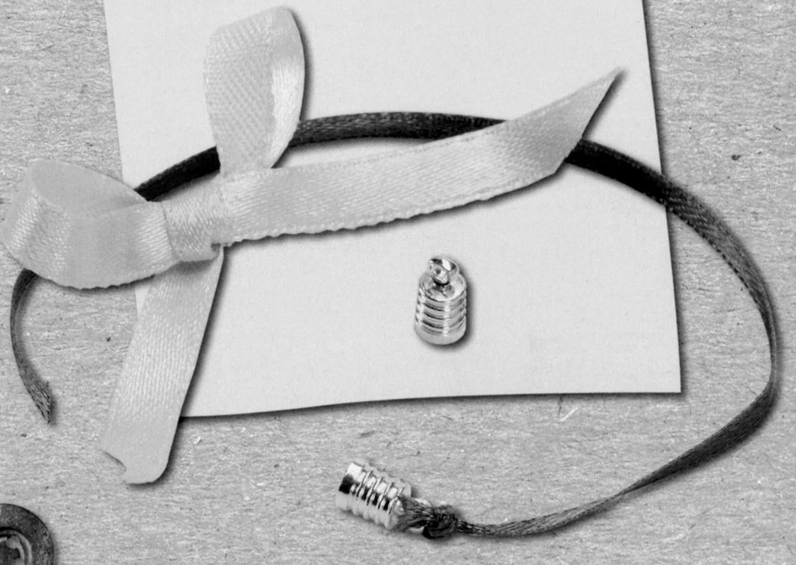

There are countless different styles of buttons, so this little bracelet can be truly unique!

5

Attach the buttons to the ribbon using a needle and thread.

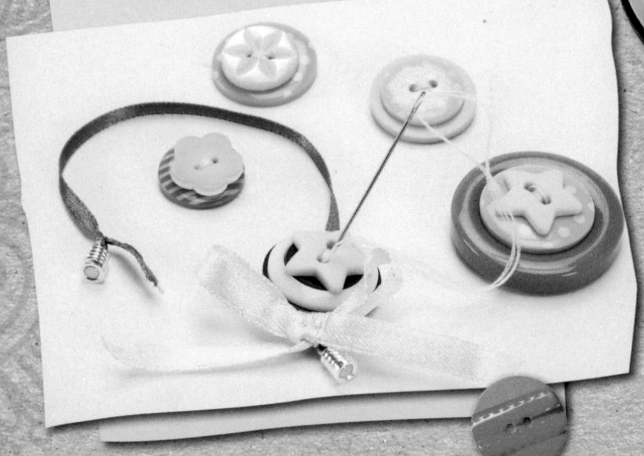

Mobile phone charm

Everyone loves their mobile phone, so why not decorate it with its own personal jewellery? This fun accessory is made from homemade scrap paper beads, but if you have a broken necklace or bracelet, you could reuse the beads from that, too.

1

Cut the scrap paper into long, flared strips approximately 20 cm long, 1 cm wide at the top, 2.5 cm at the bottom.

2

Coat a strip of paper in a thin layer of glue, then wrap it around the cocktail stick, starting with the wider end of the strip. Repeat with the other strips of paper.

3 Leave the beads to dry slightly before gently sliding off the cocktail sticks. Leave them in a warm place to dry completely.

The art of rolling paper is called 'quilling'. People make the most amazing flowers using this method!

4 Knot the string or elastic at one end, then, using the needle, thread on the beads to a length of about 10 cm. Tie another knot to keep the beads in place, then tie a loop in the remaining string or elastic.

Upgrade?

Mobile phones are made using rare and precious metals such as tungsten and cobalt. These metals can only be found in very few areas in the world and need to be mined. It's worth reconsidering upgrading your mobile phone regularly to avoid the impact this has on the environment. If you do choose to upgrade or replace your phone, there are many websites online that recycle your old phone for you. They may even pay you for your old handset!

5 Attach the charm to your mobile phone or mobile phone cover using the loop.

Friendship anklet

This classic token of friendship is great turned into an anklet rather than the more traditional bracelet. Make it extra special by making it from strips of fabric, ribbon or wool and beads that have special significance – for example from a well-loved old top that's too old and shabby to wear, or a favourite necklace that's now broken.

1

Cut the ribbon, wool or fabric strips into three pieces, each about 30 cm long.

2

Knot together the three lengths of your chosen material at one end and start plaiting them. After every two or three loops, thread a bead onto one of the lengths.

3

Cut one or two lengths of fabric, ribbon or wool for each bead you have threaded onto the plait. Using a darning needle, feed one or two lengths each through a bead.

4

Thread beads onto every length and tie a knot to keep them in place.

Once you have made an anklet for your friend, you can teach them how to make one for you!

Throughout history, wooden beads have held a symbolic meaning. In some cultures they are used in prayers; in some civilisations they can be a symbol of rank.

Reclaiming wool

Rather than buying new wool, why not reclaim some from old clothing? If you haven't got any worn-out jumpers or scarves, check out your local charity shop or ask a knitter for their old balls of leftover wool.

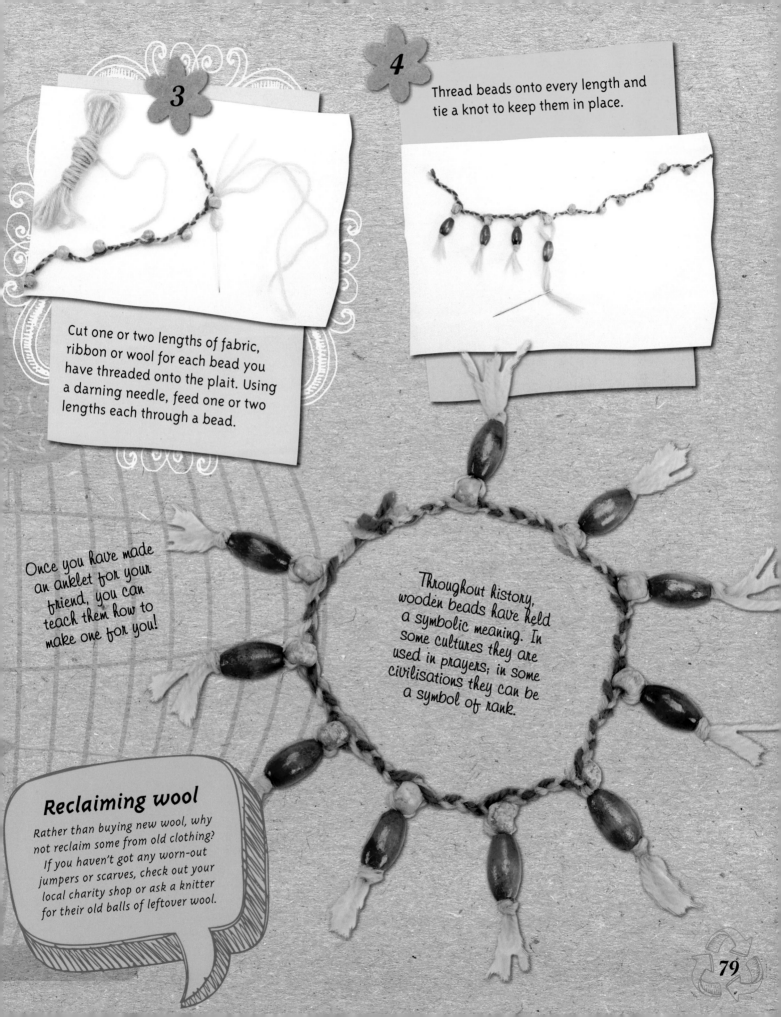

Not any old hair band

Transform a boring old Alice band into something spectacular by embellishing it with ribbons, sequins and buttons – or whatever else takes your fancy! Who needs a tiara when they could be showing off this beautifully customised hair band?

1

Wrap a strip of ribbon or fabric around the hair band, securing it in place using glue.

2

Cut leaf and petal shapes out of the foam sheets.

3

Glue the foam sheet shapes together and decorate them with buttons, beads or sequins.

4

Glue the flowers and leaves onto the hair band. Leave to dry.

You can use any material that is sturdy and colourful to create these shapes.

Make a style statement!

Accessorising with jewellery is one of the classic ways to really make a style statement. Whether you like it big and sparkly or subtle and subdued, the way you wear your jewellery says a lot about your mood!

Do you want to light up the room like a mirror ball with multiple bits of jewellery or make an impression with a subtle outfit and single statement piece such as an outrageous fascinator? Do you like everything to have a bit of glitzy glamour, or do you like things cute and pretty? Are you a tomboy at heart who still likes the bit of bling a mobile charm can give you, or are you the ultimate girly girl who wants sparkle, sparkle, sparkle?

Express yourself

Accessorise your look according to how you feel. The joy of jewellery is that you can use it to express the inner you and you can change it often. And when you make it yourself it has even more of a personal touch. Be flamboyant, be daring, be pretty, be as practical as you want to be. Think about how you feel today, then raid your jewellery box and dare to express yourself.

You can find inspiration in movies or from your favourite celebrities. You can go on the internet and look at lots of different types of accessories and create a scrapbook of what you like. You can even raid your mum's or grandmother's old jewellery collections (with their permission!) and see what might have been fashionable in the past. Old and broken jewellery can also sometimes be fashioned into something new and unique!

It's all about you! This stunning watch strap looks better than the ones you can buy, and it cost next to nothing. Best of all, its unique!

82

Design your own

You can reclaim, recycle and reuse so many materials... The only limits are your imagination!

Once you've mastered the basic projects in this book, think about how you could reuse those skills to design your own jewellery pieces. Create an embellished necklace using the same skills used for the charm bracelet on pages 60–61, or create a show-stopping hairpiece with a floral theme using the same basic techniques used for the fascinator on pages 66–67. Make a matching arm cuff to go with the choker on pages 70–71, or make a beaded keyring using the same skills used for the mobile phone charm on pages 76–77.

The Ugly Truth

Although we all love beauty products that make us feel pretty and pampered, there are some ugly facts behind their production. The average pamper product contains a wealth of chemicals and substances that can harm the environment.

Many products such as soap, bubble bath, shampoo, body lotion, lipstick, eyeliner and hair gel all include ingredients derived from petroleum. Not only is petroleum a non-renewable resource, the products it is made into are not biodegradable and so cannot break down naturally.

Another culprit is the antibacterial ingredients that are often found in soaps and cleansers. They do not break down in the environment and contribute to water pollution.

Packaging alert!

It's not just the lotions and potions we buy that can pose a threat to the environment. Stop for a moment and think about the packaging they come wrapped up in. Little feels so luxurious as a gorgeous new cleanser or bath milk in a shiny bottle nestled in a cardboard box, tied up with ribbon and shrink-wrapped in cellophane. But is all that packaging really necessary? Most of it is destined for the landfill site unless we choose to recycle, reclaim and reuse everything. And even if we do recycle, reclaim and reuse… do we really need all that packaging in the first place?

Making your own

It's incredibly easy to make your own beauty and pamper products at home and the benefits are obvious to see. By making your own, you avoid all the packaging waste that comes with commercial products. You will need containers to store products in, you can easily make beautiful, permanent ones yourself from reclaimed or re-used materials.

Many of the appealing scents of bought products are from natural ingredients you can find in your own kitchen — coconut, citrus fruits, herbs and spices. You can create your own fabulous, biodegradable products yourself naturally without chemicals and preservatives. This is good news for the environment and for your body!

Good news!
You can make all these fab crafts from stuff that usually gets thrown out!

Don't be trashy — recycle!

Make the right choices

When you buy products, always look at the label. Go for products that are organic, biodegradable and describe themselves as eco-friendly. Check that they are made from natural ingredients rather than chemicals. Choose products with the least packaging, and those packaged in recycled materials. Also make sure the products carry the recycle symbol so you know you can recycle them yourself once the product is finished.

Wonderful wash bag

Make this super cool drawstring wash bag to keep all your beauty products in. Go pretty and practical using an old shower curtain for the main fabric, then line with more luxurious satin. If you can't find suitable fabric at home, look in charity and second-hand shops. Lining fabric from an old coat is an ideal place to look for satin.

2

Place a square of satin on top of a square of shower curtain and sew the two together using a running stitch (see page 110). Repeat using the remaining two squares.

1

Cut two 22 cm x 22 cm squares from the shower curtain, and two 21 cm x 21 cm squares from the satin.

Fruity face mask

This super-simple creamy face mask made with avocado, strawberries and honey will leave your skin smooth, soft and glowing.

Scoop the flesh from one avocado into a bowl, add three strawberries and mash together to make a smooth, creamy mixture. Stir in 1/2 tsp clear honey then smooth the mask over your face.

Sit back and relax for 10 minutes, then rinse off well with warm water and pat dry with a soft towel.

3

Cut out a decorative shape such as a heart or star from the remaining satin material and sew on to one of the shower curtain squares. You can add a few cute buttons, too.

4

Place the two squares together with the shower curtain sides facing each other. Sew along the sides and bottom, leaving a 3 cm space at the top. Fold the top down and sew along the edge of the fabric to create a channel through which to thread the ribbon or cord.

5

Get ready for your next sleepover, your friends will love this!

Turn the bag inside out so the seams are on the inside. Thread one or two ribbons through each channel. Tie the ends of the ribbons at either side of the bag together in a knot.

Bath~tastic bath flannel

You will need

★ two or three old towels
★ scissors
★ needle and thread
★ ribbon

Old towels can get pretty shabby after years of use. But with a bit of creative flair you can turn an old towel into a gorgeous, good-as-new bath flannel! Simply cut your old towel into flannel-sized squares and embellish with a pretty trim and decorative shapes.

2 Using running stitch (see page 110), sew the star onto a towel of a different colour. Then cut around the star, leaving a 5 mm border.

1 Cut an 18 cm x 18 cm square from one of the towels, as well as a star, less than a quarter of the size of the square.

Rose and coconut bath soak

Make a fabulously luxurious bath soak out of simple ingredients from the kitchen. It has all the moisturising, relaxing properties of a traditional bubble bath but none of the potential damaging effects of the soaps and chemicals many bubble baths contain.
Run a bath, then add 1 tbsp rosewater and 1 tbsp coconut milk. Sit back and relax!

3

Use whipping stitch (see page 111) to attach the star to the square of towel.

4

Cut four strips from a towel, each 20 cm long and 5 cm wide. Ruffle each strip to fit the along a side of the towel square and attach it using running stitch (see page 110).

The colours on this flannel could be reversed so it's dark with white edges. Why not make a contrasting set?

Luscious lip balm

Lip balm is easy to make yourself and it looks stunning stored in this pretty decorated pot. You'll need an extra-small container, so look out for old lip balm pots or tiny jars used for make up samples. An old eye shadow container could also be ideal. Just make sure you clean and dry the container really well before you fill it with the lip balm mixture.

You will need

For the pot:
* ★ scrap paper
* ★ scissors
* ★ double-sided tape
* ★ small pot
* ★ PVA glue
* ★ button

For the lip balm:
* ★ small pan
* ★ heatproof bowl (that will sit on top of the pan)
* ★ 1 tbsp beeswax
* ★ 1 tbsp olive oil
* ★ 1 tbsp clear honey

2

Stick the strips of paper onto the container lid. Cut short pieces off the strips to stick onto the side of the container.

1

Choose some brightly coloured pages from magazines or colourful pieces of scrap paper. Cut about 10-12 narrow strips and stick them onto double-sided tape.

Lip balm

Pour about 3 cm of water into a pan. Place the bowl on top, making sure it doesn't touch the water. Put the beeswax, oil and honey in the bowl. Then heat gently until the ingredients have melted. Stir well to combine, then pour into your lip balm pot. Leave to set. Use within three months.

3

Cut petal shapes out of the scrap paper or magazine pages. You can stick slightly smaller petals onto slightly larger ones for a layered effect.

Take care when heating the lip balm ingredients – they get very hot. You may want to ask an adult to help you.

4

Stick the petals together to form a flower and glue the button in the middle. When the flower has dried, stick it onto the lid of the container. Curl the tips of the petals up.

Why not add a drop of vanilla essence to your lip balm mixture to give it a delicious scent!

Perfumed potpourri

Wood shavings

If your parents like to do a bit of DIY at the weekend, they may well have a bagful or two of wood shavings that will be perfect for this project. If they don't, ask them to take you down to your local timber merchants and ask if they have some. There should be plenty on the floor that they'll be happy to give away!

A bowl of gorgeously scented potpourri looks really pretty on any dressing table or bathroom window sill and will make the air sweet and fragrant. Make this funky bowl from scratch out of papier mâché, then fill it with your very own homemade potpourri. Using natural essential oils is much better for the environment than toxic, non-biodegradable chemicals.

You will need

- ★ balloon
- ★ PVA glue
- ★ tissue paper
- ★ scissors
- ★ paintbrush
- ★ the cardboard ring from a roll of packing tape
- ★ wood shavings and/or dried flower petals and dried twigs
- ★ scented oil, such as rose or lavender

1

Blow up the balloon and tie a knot in it. Mix 3 parts PVA glue with 1 part water.

2

Cut the tissue paper into pretty shapes. You will need many sheets' worth of shapes, so you might want to fold the tissue paper a few times before cutting out a shape.

3

Place the balloon upright into a glass or cup. Apply glue to the shapes and stick them onto the rounded half of the balloon. Apply at least three layers of the shapes.

4

Place the cardboard ring onto the top of the balloon. Attach it by sticking strips of tissue around its inside and outside edges. Once the papier mâché is dry, burst the balloon and remove it.

Potpourri was used in France as long ago as the 17th century! Ingredients used included cedar, cinnamon, cloves, juniper and lavender.

Fill a plastic bag with the wood shavings or petals, add scented oil and shake the bag to spread the mixture. Then place your potpourri your funky bowl!

Pampering pom pom

This groovy bath pom pom is a must for every girl's shower or bath. Use it to gently rub over your skin to exfoliate and leave you with glowing arms and legs. Rinse after use and you can use it again and again! You can re-use old net curtains or netting from an underskirt to make the pom pom. If you don't have anything suitable at home, take a trip to your local charity shop.

2

Fold each rectangle in half and stack them, alternating the side on which you place the folded edge.

1

Cut the netting into about twelve 5 cm x 30 cm rectangles.

3

Using needle and thread, firmly stitch the layers together in the centre of the rectangles.

4

Tie the cord or ribbon around the middle of the rectangles, pulling very tightly and knotting well. Tie the end of the cord or ribbon together to make a loop. Then fluff the netting to create the pom pom shape.

This pom pom makes a fab present for your friends, too!

Make your own body scrub

Get smooth, tingling skin using this simple mixture of kitchen ingredients. It's perfect for the summer when you're wearing shorts and T-shirts and want your skin to look at its best. Sea salt is a natural exfoliant, while ginger warms and improves circulation and olive oil gently moisturises.

Put 2 tbsp sea salt, 1 tbsp grated fresh root ginger, grated rind of 1 lemon, 1/4 peeled cucumber and 1 tbsp olive oil in a blender. Blend together then gently rub onto your legs or arms in a circular motion. Rinse off with warm water and pat dry.

95

Homemade hair gel

Create your own salon style with this very cool and very simple homemade hair gel. You even get to make a customised pot for it! Store the hair gel in the fridge and use within a week.

1

Cut the purple tissue paper into wave shapes and cut small squares out of the blue tissue paper.

2

Glue the shapes onto the side of the pot using the PVA glue and a paintbrush. Wash the paintbrush as soon as you have finished.

Why not make pretty customised pots for your shop-bought cosmetics, too?

3

Peppermint hair gel

Stir the gelatine into the warm water until completely dissolved. If you want a scented hair gel, add 2-3 drops of peppermint oil to the mixture. Pour the mixture into the customised pot and chill in the fridge for about five hours until set.

Tear up blue tissue paper into small pieces and soak in cold water for about an hour until it's very soft. Squeeze out most of the water, then mix in just enough PVA glue to make a thick, doughy paste. Mould the paste into a wave shape and leave to dry.

4

Glue the wave to the pot lid and decorate with glitter glue.

Lavender bag

Hang this scented lavender bag on a hanger in your wardrobe to make your clothes smell divine! Choose pretty fabrics from an old dress, shirt or skirt, and look out for ribbon from cosmetics packaging.

1 Using the fabrics, cut out two heart shapes (about 12 cm wide), two bird shapes (one slightly smaller than the other) and a wing shape.

2 Using whipping stitch (see page 111), sew the bird shapes onto one of the hearts and the wing shape onto the bird.

How to dry lavender

Lavender has a beautiful, strong fragrance and is ideal for drying. If you have a lavender bush at home, simply pluck off some of the flower heads and arrange on a baking sheet. Leave in a warm dry place such as a sunny windowsill to dry completely.

If you don't have your own fresh lavender to dry, you can buy dried lavender from health food stores.

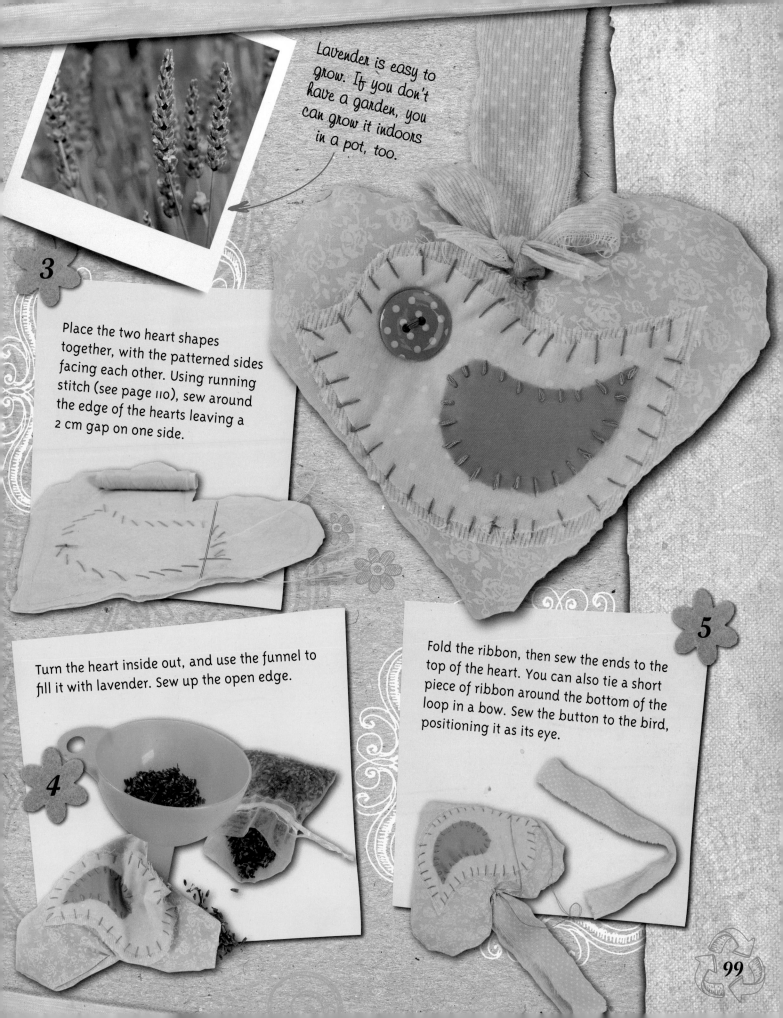

Lavender is easy to grow. If you don't have a garden, you can grow it indoors in a pot, too.

3

Place the two heart shapes together, with the patterned sides facing each other. Using running stitch (see page 110), sew around the edge of the hearts leaving a 2 cm gap on one side.

4

Turn the heart inside out, and use the funnel to fill it with lavender. Sew up the open edge.

5

Fold the ribbon, then sew the ends to the top of the heart. You can also tie a short piece of ribbon around the bottom of the loop in a bow. Sew the button to the bird, positioning it as its eye.

Funky fish soap dish

It can be hard to think of a good use for old CDs, but here's a great way to keep them out of the bin! They're shiny, waterproof and round – just perfect for turning into a glitzy, cute soap dish with a fishy theme.

You will need

★ foam sheets in various colours
★ scissors
★ pen
★ craft glue (make sure it's suitable for glueing plastic)
★ 2 used CDs
★ 4 old dice

2 Stick some small squares of foam onto the ring. Then stick the fins, tail and mouth onto one of the CDs. Stick the ring, eyes and any other shapes you want on the top of the soap dish onto the other CD.

1 Draw the shapes for your fish (fins, tail, mouth and eyes) onto the foam sheets. Using a CD as a template, draw a ring that has a 1 cm boarder. Cut all the shapes out.

Make your own soap

Instead of throwing out those tiny nubs of soap that are always left over from a bar, save them up in a jar ready to turn into a whole new bar!

To make your own soap, make sure your scraps of soap are dry. Grate them into a bowl, then add 1 tsp water at a time, stirring well until the mixture becomes soft enough to press into a ball. If the mixture is crumbly you need a little more water; if it is too soft, grate in a little more soap. Shape the mixture and leave to dry for a week before using.

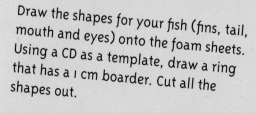

100

3

Stick the decorated discs together, so that the fin, mouth and tail shapes are between the two CDs.

4

Stick the four dice to the bottom CD.

We used groovy dice for the feet, but cut up corks will work well, too.

Why not try different animal themes for your soap dish? How about an octopus or a shark?

A bath infusion

These pretty bags, filled with fragrant herbs known for their relaxing properties, are a wonderful, natural way to scent your bath water. Once you've used the bag, simply empty the herbs into the compost, rinse out the bag and leave to dry, ready to fill with more herbs when the mood takes. You can use old net curtains, very thin cotton or an old baby muslin to make the bags.

You will need

For the bags:
* ★ cardboard
* ★ paper plate
* ★ thin cotton or muslin
* ★ scissors
* ★ needle and thread
* ★ ribbon

For the infusion:
* ★ 1 tbsp dried lavender flowers
* ★ 1 tbsp dried chamomile flowers

1 Place the paper plate on the cardboard and draw around it. Cut out the shape to use as a template.

2 Use the template to draw four circles on the muslin or cotton.

3

Cut the circles out.

4

Fold the edge of each circle inwards and use running stitch (see page 110) to create a hem of about 2 cm.

For a relaxing bath, add a fragrance bag to the hot water, plus a cup of milk.

5

Thread ribbon onto a needle and thread it through the 'channel' of the hem. Fill each bag with dried chamomile and lavender flowers and draw closed with the ribbon.

Bath bomb gift box

You will need

For the gift box:

★ tracing paper or greaseproof baking paper

★ used wrapping paper

★ thin cardboard

★ glue

★ ruler

★ ribbon

★ scissors

For the bath bombs:

★ 1 cup bicarbonate of soda

★ 1-2 tsp vegetable oil

★ 1/2 cup citric acid

★ spray bottle filled with water

★ large glass or ceramic bowl

★ spoon

★ mould, such as heart-shaped ice cube tray or small yogurt pot

★ essential oil, such as peppermint, lavender or rose

M ake these fantastic fizzing bath bombs using everyday kitchen ingredients, which makes them environmentally friendly as well as fun to use! You will be able to find most of the ingredients in health food shops. Your bath bombs will make beautiful gifts, wrapped up in this fab gift box.

1 Using tracing paper, transfer the shape of the template at the back of this book onto the cardboard.

2 Score the folds (dotted lines on the template), using the ruler and a dried up ball point pen. This will make the box easier to fold. Then cut out the shape and stick it onto the wrapping paper. Trim the wrapping paper.

3

Fold the box and stick the sides together using glue.

Bath bombs

Combine the bicarbonate of soda and citric acid in the bowl. Add about 10 drops of essential oil and the vegetable oil and stir well. Spray a tiny bit of water over the mixture and stir well. Continue gradually adding a spritz of water and stirring until the mixture has a soft and doughy consistency. Press the mixture into the moulds and leave to dry until hard. Then pop them into your gift box!

Why not try adding a little glitter to the bath bombs — sparkle-tastic!

4

Fold the base of the box as shown in the picture below. Tie the ribbon around your box for a pretty finishing touch.

Groovy grooming!

Make your own vanity kit and store it in this clever folding vanity tray! Use fabric from an old dress or skirt or an old curtain to make the vanity tray. You can also upcycle your old hairbrush with a lick of paint and some sequins from old clothes.

1 On the cereal packet, mark one 14 cm x 20 cm rectangle; two 8 cm x 14 cm rectangles; and two 8 cm x 20 cm rectangles. Cut them out.

2 Cut out a rectangle of fabric about 32 cm x 36 cm. Place the large rectangle in the centre and arrange the smaller rectangles along each edge leaving a 5 mm gap between each rectangle. Stick the rectangles onto the fabric, using the double-sided tape.

3 Place another rectangle of fabric (also measuring 32 cm x 36 cm) over the cardboard pieces. Use pins to attach the top fabric to the bottom one.

4

Use whipping stitch (see page 111) around the edges to sew the two fabric rectangles together. Then use running stitch (see page 110) to sew along the gaps between the cardboard rectangles.

5

Sew the end of a piece of ribbon (about 18 cm long) to the spots where each running stitch seam meets the edge of the fabric. You can also sew a button onto the ribbon to add a pretty finish. Then fold up the sides of the tray and tie the ribbons together at the corners.

To upcycle your old brush, use left-over paint and stick on some sequins when the paint has dried.

Throw a pamper party!

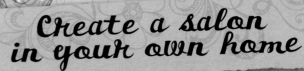
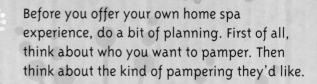

Create a salon in your own home

Soothe your senses!

W hether you're spoiling your mum and giving her a pamper treat, or inviting your friends round to recreate the spa experience – there's no end to the fun you can have with eco-friendly, homemade pamper products.

Before you offer your own home spa experience, do a bit of planning. First of all, think about who you want to pamper. Then think about the kind of pampering they'd like.

If it's your mum, she might really enjoy a bit of peace and quiet, so how about running her a hot bath and giving her the choice of a rose and coconut bath soak (page 88) or relaxing bath infusion (pages 102-103). Make sure the bathroom's really clean and tidy, then organise some relaxing music, maybe some dim lighting or candles (although check she's happy with you lighting candles before you do!), a relaxing cup of tea, a magazine and then leave her to soak in your home-made scented bath.

If you want to entertain your friends, they might enjoy having a group facial and manicure. You could whiz up the face pack (page 86) in the kitchen together, then help each other apply the mask before you sit back and file your nails while the treatment works its magic!

You could give your friend or mum a nice massage with your own homemade aromatherapy oil. You can make this by using a carrier oil, such as olive oil or jojoba oil, with a few drops of lavender or camomile oil. You can buy essential oils like these from a health food shop or a chemist.

The wash bag (pages 86–87) could make a cute party beauty bag

Party packs

If you're throwing a party for friends, why not put together some beauty bags for them to take home? Dry products such as bath bombs, soap or scented infusion bags make ideal gifts. Reuse pretty gift boxes or bags and tie them with ribbon to really make an impact. Alternatively, make your own gift boxes or bags from old wrapping paper and reused ribbon.

Craft skills

How to thread a needle

Cut a length of thread. Make sure it is no longer than your arm; too long a piece of thread will become knotted and make sewing hard work. Pass the tip of the thread through the eye of the needle. If the ends are frayed, dampen them slightly. Hold the two ends of thread together and loop into a knot. Doubling up the thread will help to make your sewing stronger.

Starting and finishing a line of stitching

To start, fasten the thread to the fabric using a few backstitches. End a line of tacking with one backstitch or a knot.

Sewing on buttons

Buttons usually have two or four holes, or have a single loop underneath. They need to be sewn on very firmly with plenty of stitches as they are generally subject to lots of wear and tear.

For a two-hole or looped button, sew through the holes or loop onto the fabric about six times in the same direction. Tie off on the underside of the fabric.

For a four-hole button, use the same technique as for the two-hole button, using opposite holes to make a cross pattern.

Tacking stitch

This is used to hold the fabric in position while it is being permanently stitched and is ideal for gathering fabric into ruffles. Pass the needle in and out of the fabric in a line to make long, even stitches.

To make ruffles, do not tie off the line of stitching. Gently pull the thread, sliding the fabric together into gathers or ruffles. When you have created the desired effect, tie off with a backstitch or knot.

Running stitch

Similar to the tacking stitch, the running stitch uses smaller stitches. It is used for seams and for gathering and can also be used to decorative effect, particularly with wool or embroidery thread. You can stitch lines or curling patterns onto the surface of fabric.

Pass the needle in and out of the fabric in small, even stitches.

Whipping stitch

This stitch is used to secure two pieces of fabric together at the edges.

Place two pieces of fabric on top of each other.

Fasten the thread to the inside of one piece of fabric. Pass the needle through both pieces of fabric from underneath, passing through where you have fastened the thread. Stitch through from the underside again to make a diagonal stitch about 1 cm from the first stitch. Repeat.

Blanket stitch

This is a decorative stitch used to bind the edge of fabric. Use a contrasting coloured thread for maximum effect.

Fasten the thread on the underside of the fabric, then pass the needle from the underside. Make a looped stitch over the edge of the fabric but before you pull it tight, pass the needle through the loop. Repeat.

Glossary

Biodegradable: type of waste that can breakdown naturally on its own

Boudoir: French for a lady's bedroom or dressing room

Combustible: capable of catching fire and burning

Concertina: an instrument with a folded shape

Consumer: a person who buys products and services for personal use

Contaminant: a toxic or poisonous substance that infects or soils other substances

Eco: often used in front of words to imply a positive effect on the environment, for example 'eco-friendly' and 'eco-fashion'

Environment: the natural world, including air, soil, water, plants and animals

Ethics: the standards of right and wrong; if something is unethical, it is deemed to be morally wrong or unacceptable

Landfill: also known as a rubbish tip or dump, landfill is a site used for the disposal of waste materials

Mining: to dig coal, metal, precious stones and other resources out of the ground

Recycle: to use something again, usually after processing or remaking in some way

Scavenge: to search for and collect

Toxic: poisonous

Upcycle: to take something that is disposable and transform it into something of greater use and value

Useful websites

ebay.co.uk an auction website where you can bid on other people's unwanted goods and possessions.

envirofone.com: a website that will pay for your old phone so that they can recycle it.

etsy.com a website where people can buy and sell handmade crafts. A great source for craft inspiration.

Folksy.com a website where people can buy, sell and learn how to make handmade crafts.

pinterest.com: a website that allows you to create visual bookmarks of your favourite things for inspiration.

recyclethis.co.uk an inspirational website with ideas on how to recycle, reuse and upcycle things that would otherwise go in the bin.

Index